Comparing
People From
the Past

Elizabeth I and
Queen
Victoria

Nick Hunter

raintree
a Capstone company — publishers for children

Raintree is an imprint of Capstone Global Library Limited, a company incorporated in England and Wales having its registered office at 7 Pilgrim Street, London, EC4V 6LB – Registered company number: 6695582

www.raintreepublishers.co.uk
myorders@raintreepublishers.co.uk

Edited by Clare Lewis and Linda Staniford
Designed by Philippa Jenkins
Original illustrations © Capstone Global Library Ltd 2015
Illustrated by HL Studios, Witney, Oxon
Picture research by Gina Kammer
Production by Victoria Fitzgerald
Originated by Capstone Global Library Ltd
Printed and bound in China

ISBN 978 1 406 28989 3
18 17 16 15 14
10 9 8 7 6 5 4 3 2 1

British Library Cataloguing in Publication Data
A full catalogue record for this book is available from the British Library.

Acknowledgements
We would like to thank the following for permission to reproduce photographs: Alamy: © INTERFOTO, 16; Bridgeman Images: © The FORBES Magazine Collection, New York/The Coronation of Queen Victoria (1819-1901) (oil), Jennens, L. (fl.1830-97) and Bettridge, H. (fl.1830-1900), 6, Private Collection/Arrival of Queen Elizabeth I at Nonsuch Palace, 1598 (hand coloured copper engraving) (detail of 324184), Hoefnagel, Joris (1542-1600), 14, Yale Center for British Art, Paul Mellon Collection, USA/A True Description of the Naval Expedition of Francis Drake, who with Five Ships Departed from the Western Part of England on 13th December 1577, Circumnavigated the Globe and Returned on 26th September 1580 with One Ship Remaining, the Others Having been Destroyed by Waves of Fire, c.1587 (pen, ink and wash on vellum), Drake, Sir Francis (c.1540-96), 20; Corbis: © Joel W. Rogers, 5, © Leemage, 28, The Gallery Collection, 4; Getty Images: De Agostini Picture Library/DEA PICTURE LIBRARY, 17, Hulton Archive/Imagno, cover (left), Hulton Royals Collection/Hulton Archive, 18, 19, 27, The Bridgeman Art Library/English School, 21, The Bridgeman Art Library/Franz Xavier Winterhalter, 13, The Bridgeman Art Library/G.S. Amato, 26; Glow Images: Heritage Images/Ann Ronan Pictures, 12, 23, Heritage Images/E&E Image Library, 25, Heritage Images/The Print Collector, 24, Superstock, 9, Superstock, 10; HL Studios, 7; iStockphotos: duncan1890, cover (right); Newscom: World History Archive, 11, 22, 29; Shutterstock: allylondon, 15; julijamilaja, 1, cover (background), Marek Stefunko, 8.

Every effort has been made to contact copyright holders of material reproduced in this book. Any omissions will be rectified in subsequent printings if notice is given to the publisher.

Contents

Some words are shown in bold, **like this.** You can find out what they mean by looking in the glossary.

Who was Elizabeth I?

Elizabeth I was Queen of England, Wales and Ireland from 1558 until 1603. Elizabeth was the daughter of King Henry VIII. She was the last of the Tudor family to rule England.

This **portrait** shows Elizabeth as a rich and powerful queen.

In 1580, Sir Francis Drake captained the first English ship to sail around the world.

Elizabeth's long **reign** is remembered as a successful time in English history. English ships explored the world and discovered new lands. Elizabeth also faced enemies at home and abroad.

Who was Victoria?

Victoria was Queen of Great Britain from 1837 until 1901. She was just 18 years old when she became queen. Victoria ruled for longer than any other British king or queen before her.

Victoria was crowned Queen at Westminster Abbey, London.

The time of Victoria's **reign** is called the Victorian Age. Victorian Britain was the most powerful country on Earth. Victoria also ruled over lands around the world that were part of Britain's **empire**.

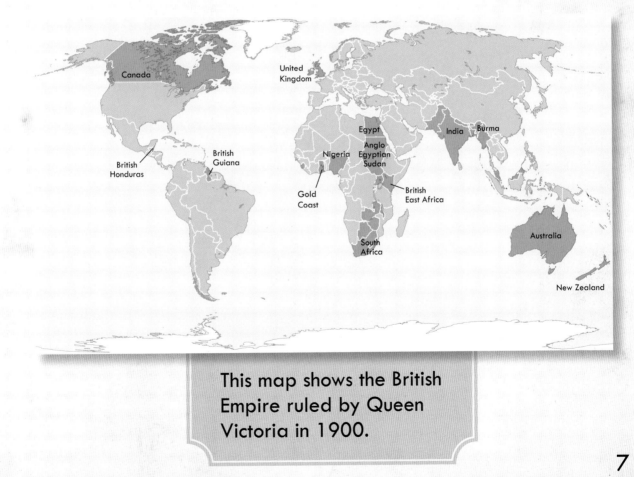

This map shows the British Empire ruled by Queen Victoria in 1900.

Family life

Elizabeth did not expect to become queen. Her brother, King Edward VI, and older sister, Queen Mary, ruled before her, but both died. Elizabeth never married and had no children of her own.

Elizabeth was locked up in the Tower of London because Queen Mary believed her sister was plotting against her.

Mary Queen of Scots was kept prisoner for many years by Elizabeth after fleeing from Scotland.

Elizabeth's cousin was also called Mary. She was Queen of Scotland. Some people thought Mary should be queen of England too. In 1587, Elizabeth had Mary **executed** after she sent secret letters to Elizabeth's enemies.

Victoria's parents were not king and queen. Her father died when she was a baby. Victoria's uncles were both kings of Great Britain but neither had children. Victoria knew she would be queen one day.

The young princess was lonely as she lived in a palace with no one to play with.

This **portrait** shows Victoria and Albert wth their children.

Victoria met her German cousin Albert when she was 17. In 1840 they were married. Victoria and Albert loved each other very much. They had a large family of nine children.

What did they wear?

It was important that Elizabeth I dressed like a queen. She owned more than 2,000 dresses, made from the finest cloths. Elizabeth loved fine jewellery, which was often given to her by her **courtiers**.

Poisonous white lead was used to make Elizabeth's face look as pale as possible, which was the fashion in those days.

In the early years of her rule, Victoria wore long dresses like this.

Queen Victoria was not very tall. When she became queen she wore heavy formal dresses with wide skirts. After the death of Prince Albert in 1861, Victoria only wore black.

Where did they live?

Elizabeth I did not live in one palace. She visited castles and grand houses around the country. She travelled with hundreds of **courtiers**. She also had many royal palaces and castles of her own.

This painting shows Elizabeth I arriving at one of her homes, Nonsuch Palace, with courtiers and servants.

A statue of Queen Victoria stands outside Buckingham Palace. This is where Elizabeth II lives today.

Victoria was the first queen to live at Buckingham Palace in London. Victoria liked staying at her homes outside London. These included Balmoral in Scotland and Osborne House on the Isle of Wight.

What did they do?

Elizabeth I was in charge of her country. Her advisers helped the Queen to govern, but Elizabeth made the final decision. Elizabeth had to be tough, as people were not used to being ruled by a woman.

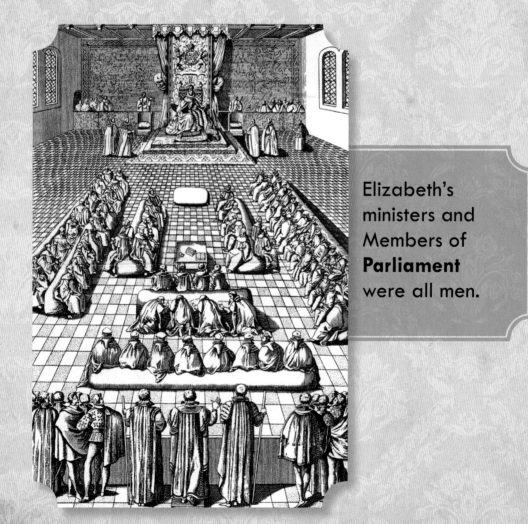

Elizabeth's ministers and Members of **Parliament** were all men.

Spain's invasion force was called the Spanish Armada.

Elizabeth's biggest challenge came from outside England. In 1588, Spain sent a huge fleet of ships to invade England. Elizabeth's navy and a fierce storm defeated them.

When Victoria was queen, laws were made by **Parliament. Prime ministers** often visited the queen to ask her advice. Victoria also enjoyed spending time with her family on holidays and festival days.

This picture shows Victoria's family celebrating around a Christmas tree, a **tradition** that Prince Albert brought from Germany.

This **portrait** was painted when Victoria was 78 years old.

After her husband died in 1861, Victoria was heartbroken. She rarely appeared in public. She dressed in black for the rest of her life. She also spent most of her time away from London.

How did Britain change?

During Elizabeth I's **reign**, famous sailors explored new lands. They brought back foods unknown in England, such as potatoes and tomatoes. They also brought back gold from raided Spanish ships.

This map shows what people knew about the world in Elizabeth's time.

Elizabeth would have watched plays in her palace rather than going to popular theatres like London's Globe.

Elizabeth's people found new ways to have fun. Theatres were opened for the first time. Elizabeth enjoyed watching the plays of William Shakespeare, which are still popular now.

The Victorian age was a time when Britain had never been more powerful. Britain's successes were shown off at the Great Exhibition of 1851. This great show was Prince Albert's idea.

The Great Exhibition was held in a giant glass building called the Crystal Palace in Hyde Park, London.

Children often had to do difficult and dangerous jobs to earn money for their families.

Most Victorians were not rich. Workers in the new factories worked long hours for little pay. Many children had to work. Later in Victoria's **reign**, most children were able to go to school.

Growing old

Elizabeth I had no children. People wondered who would rule after her. She became lonely and was seen much less by her people. As Elizabeth became ill, her **courtiers** argued about who was in charge.

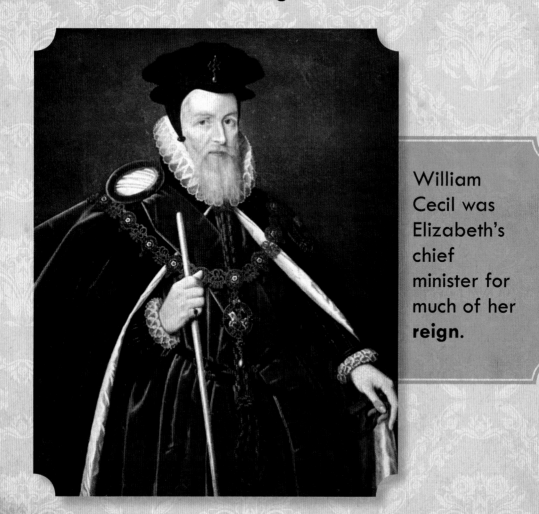

William Cecil was Elizabeth's chief minister for much of her **reign.**

Elizabeth I was buried in a grand tomb in Westminster Abbey, London.

Elizabeth died on 24 March 1603. The next king was James VI of Scotland, who became King James I of England too. James was the son of Mary Queen of Scots.

In 1897, people in Britain celebrated Victoria's Diamond Jubilee. Victoria had been queen for 60 years. There were parties across Britain and the British **Empire.**

The people celebrated
Victoria's Diamond Jubilee.

Queen Victoria
was buried at
Windsor Castle,
near London.

Queen Victoria died on 22 January 1901.
Britain had changed a lot during her
63 years as queen. Victoria's eldest son
became King Edward VII.

Comparing Elizabeth I

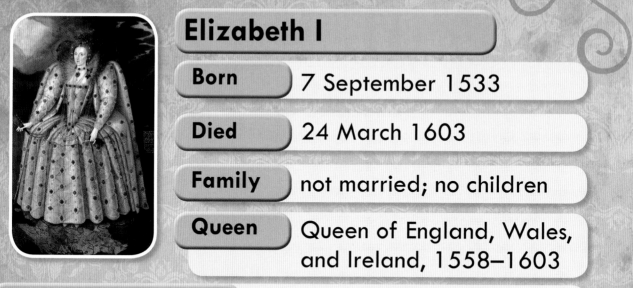

Elizabeth I

Born	7 September 1533
Died	24 March 1603
Family	not married; no children
Queen	Queen of England, Wales, and Ireland, 1558–1603

Fascinating fact

Elizabeth never met her cousin Mary Queen of Scots, although Mary was a prisoner in England for 19 years.

Famous people living at the same time

- William Cecil (Elizabeth's chief minister, 1520–1598)
- Walter Raleigh (explorer, 1552–1618)
- Francis Bacon (philosopher and scientist, 1561–1626)

ELIZABETH I

1400   1500   1600   1700

and Victoria

Victoria

Born	24 May 1819
Died	22 January 1901
Family	married Prince Albert Saxe-Coburg-Gotha in 1840; nine children
Queen	Queen of Great Britain, 1837–1901

Fascinating fact

Victoria was the first British **monarch** to have her photo taken. She was also the first to travel by train, in 1842.

Famous people living at the same time

- Isambard Kingdom Brunel (engineer, 1806–1859)
- Charles Darwin (scientist, 1809–1882)
- Florence Nightingale (nursing pioneer, 1820–1910)

QUEEN VICTORIA

1800   1900   2000

Glossary

courtier person who is part of the court of a king or queen

empire countries or lands ruled from another country

execute put to death as punishment for a crime

monarch king or queen

Parliament group of elected people who make laws

portrait picture of a person

prime minister person who leads the government of a country

reign length of time that someone is king or queen

tradition custom that has been repeated over a long period

Find out more

Books

Elizabeth I (Popcorn: People in History), Stephen White-Thomson (Wayland, 2013)

Ladybird Book of Kings and Queens of England, Louise Jones (Ladybird, 2011)

Queen Victoria (Usborne Young Reading), Susanna Davidson (Usborne, 2013)

Websites

www.bbc.co.uk/schools/primaryhistory/famouspeople/elizabeth_i/

Elizabeth I's story as told on this BBC website. It also has stories about Queen Victoria and other famous people.

www.britishpathe.com/video/diamond-jubilee-of-queen-victoria

A film showing Queen Victoria's Diamond Jubilee.

www.royal.gov.uk/HMTheQueen/TheQueenandspecialanniversaries/Factfiles/QueenVictoriasDiamondJubilee.aspx

The story of Queen Victoria's Diamond Jubilee.

Index